SCI-FI OR STEM?™

INTERSTELLAR MANNED SPACE TRAVEL

Rosen YA™
New York

JERI FREEDMAN

Published in 2019 by The Rosen Publishing Group, Inc.
29 East 21st Street, New York, NY 10010

First Edition

Library of Congress Cataloging-in-Publication Data

Names: Freedman, Jeri, author.
Title: Interstellar manned space travel/Jeri Freedman.
Description: New York : Rosen Publishing, 2019. | Series: Sci-fi or STEM? | Includes bibliographical references and index. | Audience: Grades 7–12.
Identifiers: LCCN 2017047514| ISBN 9781508180371 (library bound) | ISBN 9781508180388 (pbk.)
Subjects: LCSH: Interstellar travel—Popular works. | Manned space flight—Popular works. | Interplanetary voyages—Popular works. | Science fiction—Forecasting—Popular works.
Classification: LCC TL788.7 .F74 2019 | DDC 629.45—dc23
LC record available at https://lccn.loc.gov/2017047514

Manufactured in the United States of America

CONTENTS

INTRODUCTION

Interstellar spaceflight has long been a feature in science fiction (also called sci-fi), playing a prominent role in books, television programs, and movies. Sci-fi is a unique form of entertainment. It explores how individuals relate to and use science and speculates on how science might be used by people in the future—near or far. For this reason, science fiction is often referred to as speculative fiction. What these writers are speculating about is how the science of their day could be applied—for good or evil—in the future.

A range of technologies have been used in sci-fi to accomplish interstellar spaceflight. Some are complete fantasy, whereas others are based on scientific principles. Science fiction is predictive literature: technological aspects of the stories written by early writers were often fanciful and impossible, but sci-fi writers have actually anticipated many advances related to spaceflight. According to the European Space Agency, among such predictions (followed by the date of the works in which the technologies first appeared in print) are ultra-high-velocity projectile launchers (1865); retro-rockets (1869); planetary landers (1928); rocket fins for aerodynamic stability (1929); clustered rocket boosters (1929); the construction of orbital space stations using material delivered to

Many stories about interstellar space travel from the 1930s to the present have appeared in science fiction magazines such as *Amazing Stories*. The spaceship depicted on the May 1944 cover of the magazine has rocket fins.

the station (1945); satellite communication with the satellites in geostationary orbit (1945); and solar and light sails (1920, 1951, 1963), among other technologies. A selection of these writers, who based their concepts on the application of sound scientific principles, will be considered. Some sci-fi writers predicted applications of science that have yet to be realized, such as interstellar space travel. Could some of the elements of interstellar space travel found in sci-fi works turn out to be predictive of real scientific developments? Both the National Aeronautics and Space Administration (NASA) and privately owned companies and research organizations are exploring new technologies that could be used to power interstellar flight, so the possibility exists.

Some of these technologies use elements similar to those found in science fiction; other approaches are entirely new. All rely on an understanding of science, technology, engineering, and mathematics (STEM) disciplines. Mathematics, engineering, physics, chemistry, and biology all play a role in designing the ships and propulsion methods required for interstellar travel. Over time, as people's knowledge of space travel and its technologies expanded, the nature of interstellar space travel in science fiction changed and adapted as well. An exploration of the history of interstellar space travel in science fiction will be provided. The science and technology of prospective interstellar space travel will then be examined, along with particular organizations working in this realm and the projects they have undertaken. Technical problems that must be solved to achieve interstellar space travel and support a human population during the journey will be explained.

Human nature is less malleable than mechanical objects such as spaceships. Although humankind has developed the ability to make ever more complex—and often dangerous—machines, human nature has remained amazingly stable throughout human history. Therefore, the development of successful interstellar spaceflight would raise various practical and ethical issues. Its use would be affected by human frailties such as greed and fear. The ethical issues involved in achieving interstellar space travel will be covered as the present projects related to interstellar space and the future of interstellar space travel are explored.

CHAPTER 1

INTERSTELLAR SPACEFLIGHT IN SCIENCE FICTION

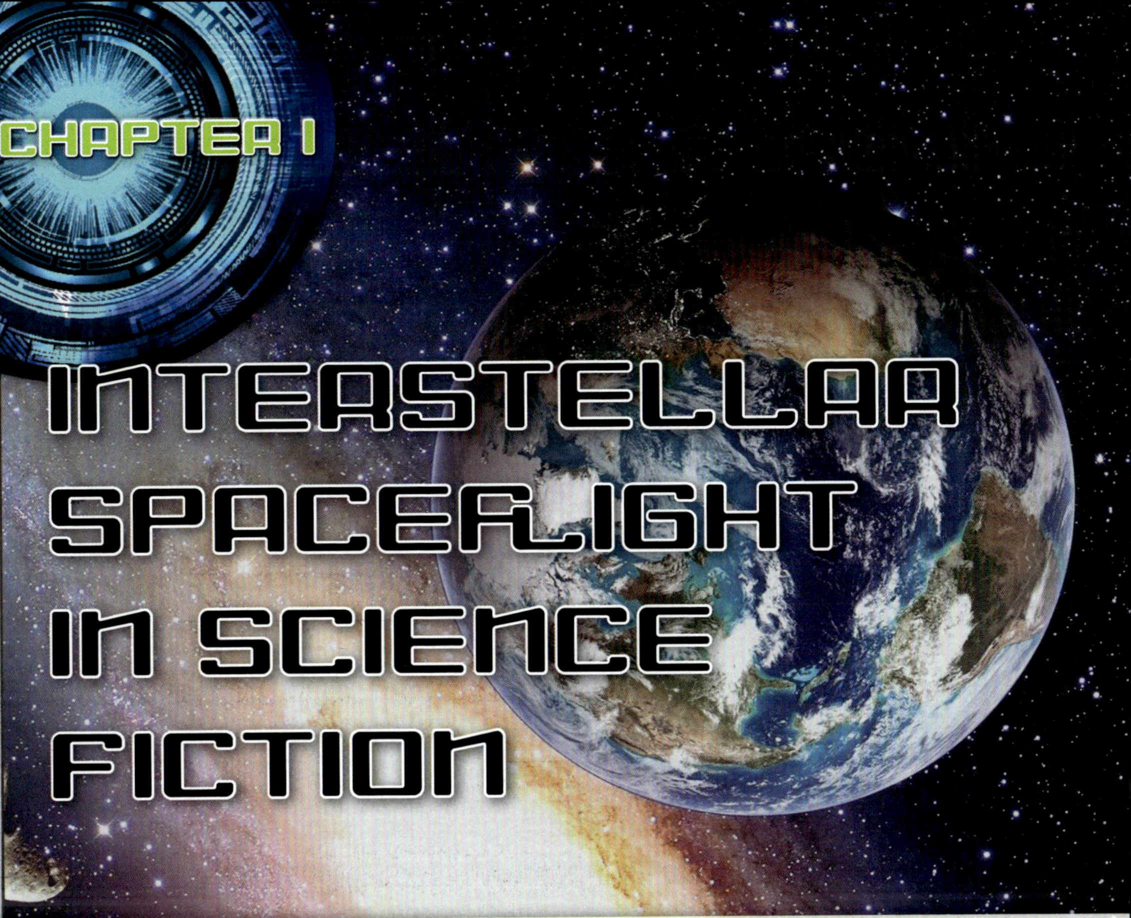

From the nineteenth century to today, interstellar spaceflight has been a cornerstone of science fiction. In some books, movies, and television shows, interstellar spaceflight is simply a mechanism to get the characters to distant galaxies where the action takes place. In other cases, the flight itself is the focus of the story.

WRITING ABOUT INTERSTELLAR FLIGHT

Before there was interstellar spaceflight in fiction, there was galactic spaceflight, travel within the Milky Way galaxy. The earliest example of this was a trip to Earth's moon. Since the

This photo of an amazing array of stars in the Milky Way galaxy was taken by the Hubble Space Telescope on its journey through space.

moon is easily visible from Earth, it naturally excited speculation among writers. In the second century CE, satirist Lucien of Samosata (circa 120 CE–after 180 CE) wrote a story in his work *A True History* in which he sets out on a voyage in a sailing ship and is caught up in a storm and carried in the ship to the moon. In 1638,

Bishop Francis Godwin wrote *The Man in the Moone*, in which a Spaniard, Domingo Gonzales, travels to the moon in a primitive machine, featuring a sail, propelled by birds. These stories are sometimes touted as sci-fi tales, but are in truth fantasy because the authors make no attempt to provide a scientific basis for the way the characters' vehicles get to the moon or for what they find when they arrive. That said, even works accepted as science fiction today often rely on unexplained or nonexistent methods of propulsion or sources of energy. So, to some extent, intention defines what is science fiction and what is fantasy. Sci-fi writers, unlike fantasy writers, make an attempt to base the characteristics of their ships on scientific principles—at least as they are understood at the time the stories were written.

In the eighteenth century, interest in science flowered, and stories incorporating science captivated people's imaginations, including stories of space travel. More than two hundred stories of flights to the moon were published in the eighteenth century. Interest in what was "up there" was not surprising during this period, when new scientific discoveries and inventions were being made throughout the world, and explorers were covering Earth in search of new lands. Dutch lens maker Isaac Newton (1642–1727) described the basic laws of physics, and mathematician and astronomer Johannes Kepler (1571–1630) wrote about the laws of celestial physics, such as those governing planetary motion. In Kepler's book *Somnium* (*The Dream*), he speculates about how Earth, other planets, and eclipses would look from the moon. Although his story is a fantasy, he based his descriptions on the science of his day, making the work, in some sense, science fiction. Stories of traveling to the moon continued through the nineteenth century, with works such as H.G. Wells's *The First Men in the Moon* (1901), into the twentieth century. By the twentieth century, spaceships in science

The main characters enter their spacecraft for their trip to the moon in H. G. Wells's *The First Men in the Moon* (1901). This illustration is from a 1913 edition that was published in London, England.

fiction were going well beyond the moon to other planets, within our galaxy and beyond.

There is a symbiotic relationship between science and stories of spaceflight in science fiction. As new scientific discoveries are made, writers are quick to adopt these principles in their stories. For example, the earliest "moon ships" were powered by wind, a form of energy with which people were familiar from sailing ships and windmills. By the nineteenth century, the machines in sci-fi stories were powered by steam—the energy that powered industrial machines and vessels such as steamships and trains. To some extent, the reverse is also true. Sci-fi writers speculate about the possible ways in which ships might cross the stars, and their ideas can provide ideas for research by scientists. One example of the influence of science fiction on reality is Edward Everett Hale's story "The Brick Moon," which was serialized in the *Atlantic Monthly* (1869). In this story, Hale describes the building of an artificial moon fixed in space above Earth so that it could be used by ships at sea to navigate. Thus, Hale anticipated the human-made satellite—and the idea of a global positioning system (GPS).

It was in the wake of the Industrial Revolution of the late nineteenth century that true science fiction developed—fiction in which science played a prominent role in the plot of the story. The second decade of the twentieth century saw the publication of the first pulp fiction magazines. Printed monthly on cheap paper, these popular magazines focused on exciting adventure stories, and greatly expanded the market for sci-fi stories. By the 1920s, these magazines were publishing stories in which spaceships featured prominently. Among such early stories were the first Buck Rogers novella, *Armageddon, 2419 A.D.*, and the first Doc Smith story, "Skylark of Space," both published in the August 1928 issue of *Amazing Stories*. The pulps continued to flourish in the 1930s and 1940s. In 1941, Robert A. Heinlein wrote two connected novellas: *Universe* (*Astounding Science-Fiction* magazine, May 1941) and its sequel, *Common Sense* (*Astounding Science-Fiction* magazine, October 1941), which were published together as the novel *Orphans of the Sky* in 1963. *Universe* is about a multigenerational ship traveling through space. So many generations live and die on the giant ship's voyage that those who inhabit it believe it is the entire universe.

World War II (1939–1945) brought with it major advances in rocket technology, indeed, in technology in general. One aspect of the Cold War between the United States and the Soviet Union was a competition between the two countries to become the leader in scientific advances: putting a satellite into orbit, orbiting Earth in a rocket, and putting a real rather than fictional man on the moon. This competition increased interest in science fiction among young people and opened new vistas for speculative fiction writers to explore. Once space travel became a reality, the stars were the

This conceptual artwork shows a possible design for a multigenerational spaceship for interstellar space travel.

limit. From the 1950s to the 1970s, writers such as Isaac Asimov, James Blish, Arthur C. Clarke, A. E. Van Vogt, and others crafted science fiction novels that incorporated interstellar spaceflight. Some of their works would become classics of the genre. Among the books of the period featuring interstellar travel are *The Stars, Like Dust* (1951) by Isaac Asimov and *Rendezvous with Rama* (1973) by Arthur C. Clarke.

In a 1984 article in the *New York Times*, "The Truth Isn't Stranger Than Science Fiction—Just Slower," sci-fi writer Isaac Asimov asked,

> What kind of mind is required to think of things to come a generation and more ahead? Nothing unusual, judging by my own. It's just a matter of knowing science and technology and the way they have developed, and of thinking what the next steps might logically be—and thinking and thinking. People expect dramatic shortcuts, but it all boils down to the dull, hard work of thought.

Through learning and applying the principles of STEM, anyone could be involved in making parts of science fiction reality.

INTERSTELLAR SPACEFLIGHT IN THE MOVIES

Not long after the means of making movies was invented, in the last decade of the nineteenth century, it was used to make a movie about a trip to the moon: French filmmaker Georges Méliès' *Le Voyage dans la lune* (*A Trip to the Moon*, 1902). Until the 1950s, however, spaceflight played only a peripheral role in science fiction films. It served simply as a method of getting characters from one place to another, without any explanation of how the ships operated. The 1950s were an era of major technological advances—not all of them positive. Rocketry and the atomic bomb excited the interest of the public, and sci-fi films flourished. In 1950, the film *Destination Moon*, whose script was cowritten by Robert A. Heinlein, attempted to provide a technically accurate version of spaceflight. In the film, an aerospace scientist, a former Air Force

SCI-FI SOURCES: SO THIS IS INTERSTELLAR SPACE TRAVEL

The following are descriptions of interstellar space travel from three sci-fi works. They provide insight into sci-fi writers' views of spaceship technology over time.

In Isaac Asimov's *The Currents of Space* (1952), the character Genro takes a space yacht for a test drive:

> The ship rolled out of the hangar like an air-borne whale, moving slowly, its diamagnetized hull clearing the smooth packed clay by three inches … The ship came to a halt, pinpointed at the lip of a take-off pit. The dia-magnetic field strengthened progressively towards the ship's prow and it began tipping upward … Majestically the ship's rear flanges fitted into the appropriate grooves of the pit. It stood upright, pointing to the sky.
>
> The duralite cover of the take-off pit slipped into its recess, revealing the neutralized lining, a hundred yards deep, that received the first energy thrusts of the hyper-atomic motors.

In Frederik Pohl's novella *The Gold at the Starbow's End* (1972), Lieutenant-Colonel Sheffield N. Jackman of the US Air Force, the commander of the first starship to leave the galaxy, records details of the voyage in his logbook:

> We are now approaching the six-week point in our expedition to Alpha Centauri, Planet Aleph … We should be crossing the orbit of Pluto at approximately 1631 hours (4:31), ship time, Day 40 … Letski has been keeping track of the time dilation effect, which is beginning to be significant now that we are traveling about some 6 percent of the speed of light … From then on we will have left the solar system behind and thus will be the first human beings to enter upon the deeps of interstellar space.

David Brin's book *Insistence of Vision* (2016) contains a starship that travels at near the speed of light. An alien the ship encounters describes its means of propulsion as follows:

> It operates by the series-implosion of micro-singularities [tiny black holes], which you create by borrowing spacetime-metric, using principles of quantum uncertainty. Before this borrowed debt comes due, you allow the singularities to re-collapse behind you. This creates a spacetime ripple, a wake that propels you ahead without any need on your part to expend matter or energy.

general, and an industrialist devise a plan to land Americans on the moon. They construct and launch a spaceship manned by four astronauts from a base in the Mojave Desert. The film was a commercial success, which encouraged studios to make more science fiction films. In 1956, Metro-Goldwyn-Mayer (MGM) released one of the classics of 1950s sci-fi movies: *Forbidden Planet*. It was the first sci-fi film to show human beings using a spaceship that could travel

A Naboo N-1 starfighter engages a Lucrehulk-class droid control ship in *Star Wars: Episode II Attack of the Clones*. Although there are many types of spacecraft in the *Star Wars* universe, not much is known about the scientific concepts propelling them through space.

at a speed faster than the speed of light to achieve interstellar space travel.

The films of the 1960s brought greater realism to science fiction. One of the epic films of the period was *2001: A Space Odyssey* (1968), written by veteran science fiction author Arthur C. Clarke and directed by Stanley Kubrick. The first *Star Wars* movie was released in 1977. It attracted a huge audience, including many people who were not typically sci-fi fans. Despite the large variety of spacecraft in the *Star Wars* universe, however, there is little explanation of the scientific principles of spaceflight that govern them.

In the last two decades of the twentieth century, action and fantastic adventure captured audiences' interest much better than science-based space flicks. While *Star Wars, Star Trek,* and the *Alien* movies proliferated, *2010*, Arthur C. Clarke's sequel to *2001: A Space Odyssey*, was a flop at the box office. In the twenty-first century, there has been a renewed interest in science-based space movies, with films such as *Gravity*, in which a pair of astronauts struggle to survive after an accident leaves them stranded in space, and *Interstellar*, in which a group of space explorers travel through a wormhole. At the same time, movies such as *Ender's Game*, the military sci-fi story based on the novel by Orson Scott Card, and the 2014 humorous adventure flick *Guardians of the Galaxy* and its 2017 sequel have continued the trend of action adventure pictures set in space.

AS SEEN ON TV

Television shows from *Space Patrol* to *Flash Gordon*, *Alien Nation*, *Battlestar Galactica*, and *Star Trek* relied on space travel as a key part of their adventures. The first sci-fi TV series were children's shows, including *Captain Video and His Video Rangers* (1949–1955), *Tom Corbett, Space Cadet* (1950–1955), and *Space Patrol* (1950–1955). *Captain Video* took place on Earth, but *Tom Corbett* and *Space Patrol* traveled the stars.

The 1960s saw the inception of sci-fi exploration shows in which space explorers traveled the galaxy and beyond, encountering a different adventure each week. *Lost in Space* (1965–1968) followed the adventures of a team of space explorers who are marooned. However, other than the convention that they had arrived at the location via spaceship, actual flight played no part in the show. The first episode of *Star Trek*, produced by Gene Roddenberry, aired in 1966, but in 1966 many people who were not dyed-in-the-wool science fiction fans found the show incomprehensible. The original series lasted only three years. The show employed established sci-fi writers to craft its stories and popularized such futuristic technologies as warp drive, replicators to produce food and other objects, phaser weapons, and a teleportation system. The show made at least an attempt to incorporate a scientific basis into its technologies. The space program increased the public's interest in and understanding of the possibilities of spaceflight, and in 1979 *Star Trek: The Motion Picture* brought *Star Trek* to the big screen for the first time. *Star Trek* familiarized the public with the idea of "warp drive" as a means of jumping from one point in space to another, far distant point. Five more movies featuring the cast of the original series followed.

Battlestar Galactica was a colony-in-space drama created by Glen A. Larson. The original series ran from 1978 to 1979. In 2003, a new version of *Battlestar Galactica* aired as a miniseries and was followed in 2004 by a regular TV series, also called *Battlestar Galactica* (2004–2009), and a year later by a prequel series, *Caprica* (2009–2010). All the *Battlestar Galactica* series are based on the idea that human civilization has expanded to colonize planets in a distant part of the universe. After a war with cybernetic aliens called Cylons, the humans are defeated, and the remnants of the population escape on *Battlestar Galactica*, a gigantic battleship. Like *Star Trek*, *Battlestar Galactica* incorporated some science into storylines about the characters and their interstellar adventures.

In 1987, *Star Trek* was revived with a new series, *Star Trek: The Next Generation* (1987–1994), which was followed by *Star Trek: Deep Space 9* (1993–1999), *Star Trek: Voyager* (1994–2001), and *Star Trek: Enterprise* (2001–2005), as well as a second series of movies in the 2000s featuring a new array of actors. In 2017, CBS premiered a new *Star Trek* series, *Star Trek: Discovery*, on its CBS All Access channel. The series and its spinoffs introduced concepts such as voice-recognition computers and masking shields for warships. *Star Trek* shaped the popular view of what interstellar space travel should be like in many ways and sparked the imaginations

In a scene from a 1978 episode of the first *Battlestar Galactica* series, the characters interact with an alien.

of a generation of young scientists, who have started investigating some of the types of technologies used on the show. While literal versions of technologies such as replicators and teleportation may not be feasible, related approaches such as using 3D food printers to create on-demand food are under development, and some technologies, such as voice-activated computers, have become reality.

CHAPTER 2

TRAVELING BY STARSHIP

Several major approaches have been employed to get characters in sci-fi stories to their destinations. Some of these methods are beyond current technological capabilities, but others are being explored by scientists and engineers. The key to traveling across vast distances of space is being able to accelerate the spaceship to near the speed of light: 186,282 miles per second (299,792,458 meters per second), which is the maximum speed at which an object can travel. Various methods have been proposed for achieving this speed or getting around this limitation.

SUSPENDED ANIMATION

A starship that travels across long distances using conventional means of propulsion might take thousands of years to reach its destination. Clearly, this method raises the problem of having the crew live long enough to make the journey. There are two common approaches to solving this problem: multigenerational ships and suspended animation.

In *2001: A Space Odyssey*, an astronaut gets in shape by jogging. Hibernation chambers, in which astronauts are placed in suspended animation, can be seen along the walkway. The movie included sounder science than most science fiction films.

Life science is the forgotten technology of space travel. Interstellar flight is often discussed in terms of physics, but a trip through space can take hundreds or even thousands of years, depending on the destination. Even after a mere fifty-year trip, the passengers would be too old to accomplish their purpose when they arrived.

One solution is to put the crew into a state of hibernation or suspended animation by means such as freezing, or cryogenics. The ship is automated, and when it arrives at the destination, the people are woken or defrosted. This approach is used in Arthur C. Clarke's *2001: A Space Odyssey* (1968), among other works. In these stories, the people usually emerge in perfect condition and ready to perform their tasks, with no explanation of how their muscle tone and strength were maintained while they were unconscious.

MULTIGENERATIONAL SHIPS

Multigenerational ships rely on participants to create successive generations of space travelers. Because many people, perhaps enough to found an entire colony (at least ten to forty thousand), will be living on the ship for a long period, such ships are usually very large. Passengers must be able to grow or make all the food and objects they will need. Thus, such ships are essentially cities in space.

IMPROBABILITY AND IMPLAUSIBILITY DRIVES

Not all sci-fi works that incorporate interstellar spaceflight rely on accepted scientific principles. In some works, particularly those with a comic bent, authors have developed unique and creative approaches to the problem. Douglas Adams's humorous book *The Hitchhiker's Guide to the Galaxy* (1979) satirizes many of the conventions of science fiction, and interstellar space travel is no exception. Adams's heroes travel the universe in a ship powered by the Infinite Improbability Drive, "a wonderful new method of crossing vast interstellar distances in a mere nothing of a second, without all that tedious mucking about in hyperspace." The drive was developed by a student after scientists repeatedly failed, deciding that developing such a drive was a "virtual impossibility."

The student reasoned that a virtual impossibility was a finite improbability. That is, if it wasn't totally impossible, it was merely extremely improbable. He fed data on just how improbable it was to a "finite improbability generator," and—poof!—an infinite improbability drive was created. The Infinite Improbability Drive works by running through every single (thus infinite) possibility in the universe until it comes up with the one the characters want—such as going to the other end of the universe.

The Infinite Improbability Drive is not the only odd means of space travel in science fiction. The Doctor in the *Doctor Who* British TV series travels by means of the Time and Relative Dimension in Space (TARDIS) device. The TARDIS, which first appeared on the show in 1963, is disguised as a police call box and is larger inside than out. It allows the Doctor to travel through both space and time. In some episodes it dematerializes and rematerializes, while in others it's used for conventional space travel. In 1996, the British Broadcasting Corporation (BBC) applied for a trademark for the TARDIS's police box image, despite the fact that the London Metropolitan Police challenged the application. In a ruling almost as absurd as the method of travel, the British Patent Office ruled that neither the Metropolitan Police nor any other police force had ever registered a patent on the police call box and awarded the BBC the trademark.

The TARDIS appears on the top of Cardiff Castle in Wales. It could travel through time as well as space.

RAMJET SCOOPS AND LIGHT SAILS

Crossing vast distances in space to arrive at even the nearest stars to Earth, such as Alpha Centauri or Barnard's Star, is going to require a spaceship that can travel at least 10 percent of the speed of light. To go beyond the nearest stars, the ship would have to travel at least 30 percent of the speed of light. To maintain this level of speed over the distance necessary would require a spaceship that uses fuel very efficiently—or, better yet, not at all. Two strategies for "fuelless" travel are light sails and ramjets. A ramjet is a type of jet engine in which fuel is injected into a stream of compressed air that shoots out the back of a ship to move it forward.

A stream of compressed air shoots out the back of a rocket (in this case a cruise missile) with a ramjet engine to propel it forward.

A ramjet scoop, or ram scoop, is a device that would create a strong magnetic field and use it as a scoop to collect interstellar hydrogen during spaceflight. The hydrogen would be directed into a fusion reactor, which would fuse the atoms together, a process that releases tremendous energy. Theoretically, a ramjet of this type could propel a starship at a speed very close to the speed of light. Practically, there are factors involved in the process, such as the drag, or friction, created by the magnetic field, that could make it somewhat slower. The spaceships in Poul Anderson's and Larry Niven's sci-fi novels rely on ramjet scoops for propulsion. Ramjet scoops won't work until a ship reaches 4 to 6 percent of the speed of light. Niven addresses this problem by having his ship use a laser-propelled light sail or standard rocket fuel to achieve a speed of from 4 to 6 percent of the speed of light, allowing the ramjet scoop to take over at that point.

Light travels in waves composed of photons—light particles. Using solar light or starlight to power a starship could eliminate the need to carry fuel. However, as with terrestrial solar power, a light sail requires a large amount of light. The farther a ship gets from the sun or another powerful star, the less efficient this mode of power becomes. Light sails are most often used in science fiction to reach a speed at which a ramjet can take over and propel the ship. This technique works well because in the earliest phase of the trip, the ship would have the greatest light from the sun or other star. Where adequate ambient light is not available, powerful ground-based lasers could be used to power up the ship. Light sails are huge, so they add significant weight to the ship, but because the ship doesn't have to carry heavy engines and fuel, it still weighs less than other types of ships.

This artwork shows an illustrator's concept of what an ion-drive spacecraft might look like.

ION AND FUSION DRIVES

In 1989, US astronaut Edward Gibson wrote a novel called *Reach* in which he described a method of propulsion that relies on an ion drive. The drive uses electricity to accelerate ions of mercury until they reach 1 percent of the speed of light and expels them from the rear of the ship to propel it forward.

Fusing two atoms into a single atom is a process called fusion. This process generates a large amount of energy. Theoretically, controlled fusion reactions could be used to power rockets. The electrically charged particles produced by the fusion reaction would be accelerated to the speed of light and expelled by the spaceship's propulsion system. One advantage of fusion drives is that they require less fuel than conventional chemical rocket propulsion. Additional "fuel," frequently consisting of bismuth atoms, can be injected into the propulsion system for more thrust. The ships in *Star Wars* use fusion drives, as do those in the Perry Rhodan sci-fi novels (a series of German space adventure novels translated into English by Wendayne Ackerman and published by Ace Books from 1969 to 1978).

FTL: WORMHOLES AND WARP DRIVES

One method in science fiction by which ships cross interstellar space with extreme speed is called faster-than-light (FTL) travel. For example, the battlestar spaceship *Galactica* (from the TV sci-fi series *Battlestar Galactica)* is propelled by a faster-than-light drive. With FTL, the ship doesn't actually move faster than the speed of light. Rather, it gets from point A to point B at a speed faster than that of light traveling on a flat path through space. It does this by taking a shortcut. The drive folds space and creates a wormhole (scientifically called an Einstein-Rosen bridge, after the scientists Albert Einstein and Nathan Rosen, who described it). The wormhole is a shortcut between two points in space. It allows a ship like the *Galactica* to reach a distant point in the universe more rapidly than light without violating the laws of physics.

The famous warp drive in *Star Trek* also folds space to jump from one point in space to another. Warp drive uses a technology known as a gravimetric field displacement manifold. The warp drive creates a subspace field around the ship, which distorts space-time. The reaction is powered by matter/antimatter reactions fueled by the element deuterium. Antimatter is the opposite of normal matter. Normal matter consists of atoms, which are composed of protons with a positive electrical charge and electrons with a negative electrical charge. Antimatter's atoms are composed of particles with the opposite electrical charges—its protons have a negative electrical charge and its electrons have a positive electrical charge. When a particle of matter and a particle of antimatter collide, the result is an explosion. A matter/antimatter reaction releases many times more energy per unit of fuel than even a nuclear reaction. The dilithium crystals referred to in the TV series focus the reactions, but they are not the fuel used to drive the ship. In real life, traveling to a far distant point probably could not be accomplished in a single "jump." It would require many jumps.

CHAPTER 3

REAL SCIENCE AND INTERSTELLAR TRAVEL

The principle by which a rocket moves in space is simple. It relies on Isaac Newton's third law of motion—for every action there is an equal and opposite reaction. This law is why, when a bullet is shot from the muzzle of a gun, the gun recoils, or pushes back against the shooter's hand. Rockets move in space by expelling some form of propellant behind them, which generates an opposite force that pushes them forward. The trick is to find a means of expelling propellant from the rear of the rocket that will move it forward at great speed. This problem is complicated by the fact that rockets can carry only a finite amount of fuel, and the system that accelerates and expels the fuel must be of a size and weight suitable for use in a spaceship. Researchers have already begun testing some of the methods described in science fiction.

A BETTER SPACECRAFT

To get to even the nearest star, people will need new types of engines and new fuels. Scientists are exploring alternate technologies to today's chemically propelled rockets.

The "atomic drive," or nuclear energy engine, was often used to power sci-fi spaceships in the 1930s. The use of nuclear bombs exploded behind a spacecraft to propel it forward was explored in the 1940s during the Manhattan Project, whose purpose was to develop the atom bomb. Two scientists working on the Manhattan Project in 1944, Stanislaw Ulam and Frederic de Hoffmann, began to investigate atomic propulsion for spaceflight. Another scientist, Frederick Reines, and Ulam worked out the calculations for the propulsion and noted them in a classified memorandum in 1947. When they applied to the US Department of Defense's Advanced Research Projects Administration (DARPA) for financial sponsorship, the US government agreed and codenamed the project Orion. The object of Project Orion was to create a space vehicle propulsion system that moved a spaceship forward by exploding atomic bombs roughly two hundred feet (sixty-one meters) behind it. Work began on Project Orion in 1958 at General Atomics (now part of General Dynamics) in San Diego, California. In 1959, the company succeeded in proving that impulse-based propulsion was possible by achieving a 109-yard (100 m) flight with a model prototype using six explosive charges.

The primary researchers on Project Orion, Theodore Taylor and Freeman Dyson, believed that nuclear-propelled rockets could carry more people and cargo than the chemical-propelled rockets being developed at the time. A ship using this technology,

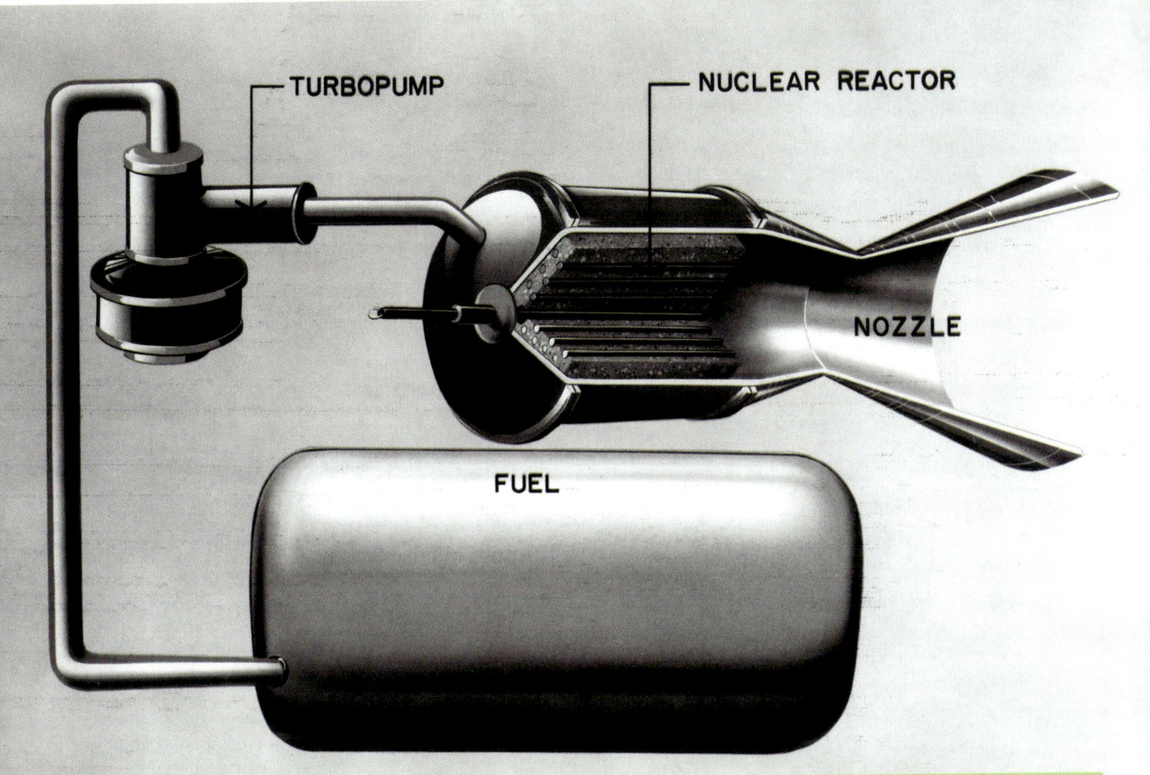

A 1945 diagram for a nuclear rocket engine depicts the fuel tank, turbopump, nuclear reactor, and nozzle.

which was to have been called Orion, would have looked more like the rocket ships described by sci-fi writers (very large multiroom ships) than the space capsules used in the early days of space exploration. However, the project ran into two problems. First, in 1958, the US government created NASA and shifted control of all nonmilitary space projects to the new agency. Orion was getting its funding from the Department of Defense, but it was not a weapon system. So the Defense Department lost interest in pursuing the project. Second, NASA shied away from using nuclear-powered spacecraft for fear of having an accident that would create adverse public opinion. When the 1963 nuclear test-ban treaty was signed by the United States, the Soviet Union, and the United Kingdom, it outlawed the exploding of nuclear bombs by all three powers. This treaty effectively made it illegal to explode the bombs necessary to propel a vehicle by this method, and the project was canceled. In 1968, Dyson wrote a paper describing nuclear-pulse drives in detail and suggesting that extremely large starships powered by fusion explosions were viable. Such ships might be more feasible today than in the 1960s because significant progress has been made in the design of nuclear bombs in the past several decades, making them smaller and more powerful. There are still political as well as technical problems to be overcome. Both environmental contamination from radiation and the danger of bombs exploding on a launch platform could be overcome, for instance, by having the vehicle transported into space and launched from a space-based platform. The technology could cut the travel time of spacecraft from 30 to 80 percent of that of chemical rockets. The drawbacks are that propulsion by nuclear fission is inefficient—it uses massive amounts of energy—and it leaves a trail of radioactive particles.

The idea of making a nuclear-fusion rocket, instead of a nuclear-fission rocket, was developed by the British Interplanetary Society (BIS). The BIS's concept for a ship, to be called *Daedalus*, consisted of an unmanned interstellar probe driven by fusion "microexplosions." To power the ship, fuel pellets would be irradiated with electron beams in a magnetic "combustion chamber," creating a plasma (a state of matter between gas and liquid). A magnetic field would be used to confine and shape plasma so that it could be used to power the ship. *Daedalus* would be vastly more efficient than *Orion*. It is quite

NASA is working on developing the *Orion* spacecraft, which would be capable of exploring deep space and Mars. In this photo, *Orion* is being loaded onto an aircraft after a spacecraft parachute test in 2013.

possible that some day nuclear propulsion will power interstellar space vehicles. The technology necessary to build an Orion-type spaceship already exists. No one has produced controlled-fusion energy using electron beams or other technology, but researchers are working on the technology to do so.

In 2011, NASA embarked on a new project for an *Orion* spacecraft with the goal of developing a ship for deep space exploration. Its first goal is to send astronauts to explore Mars. It is not, however, a nuclear-powered space vehicle like its namesake. In early 2018, the spacecraft was under construction.

THE 100 YEAR STARSHIP

DARPA and NASA have teamed up (starting in 2010) to promote a project to create a spacecraft that can reach the nearest star within one hundred years, offering a $500,000 grant for the person who can solve the problem. Various companies have taken up the challenge posed by the 100 Year Starship (100YSS) project.

One such company is Icarus Interstellar, Inc., a nonprofit group of scientists and engineers, headed by the Tau Zero Foundation and the BIS. They are working to develop a complete set of technical reports containing "the engineering layout, functionality, physics, operation, expected performance, and mission profile" for a robotic (unmanned) ship that can explore interstellar space. Icarus aims to send a craft to a nearby star, such as Proxima Centauri, a red dwarf star around four light-years from Earth, within fifty years. If Icarus succeeds, some young people may experience a spacecraft reaching another star system in their lifetime.

The leading method of propulsion considered by the Icarus team is a fusion drive. A fusion drive could propel the starship at more than 10 percent the speed of light, which would make such a trip feasible. However, the organization has yet to decide on the exact design for such a drive.

NASA's Evolutionary Xenon Thruster project is developing an ion engine that is intended to accelerate a spacecraft to speeds up to 90,000 miles per hour (145,000 kilometers per hour) using only a fraction of the fuel of a conventional rocket. Even a warp drive is not out of the realm of possibility—although it is improbable anytime soon. Harold "Sonny" White, a physicist at NASA's Johnson Space Center in Houston, Texas, has been investigating whether a warp-drive engine could be built. White is head of the

The Alpha Centauri star system, part of the constellation of Centaurus, is made up of the double stars Alpha Centauri A and Alpha Centauri B (*top left and right*) and the red dwarf star Proxima Centauri (*center*). The Proxima B planet (*bottom*) orbits Proxima Centauri, the target for NASA's first interstellar spacecraft.

center's advanced propulsion program. His team has been using a device called a White-Juday Warp Field Interferometer in an attempt to generate and detect microscopic instances of tiny warp bubbles, or distortions, in space. So far, his results have been inconclusive, but if his experiment works, it could someday lead to the development of a system that could produce a bubble of warped space-time around a spacecraft. This type of warp drive would not cause the spaceship to go faster. Rather, it would warp the space along its route, which would allow it to avoid the restriction against faster-than-light-travel.

At the other end of the spectrum, NASA is working on a solar electric propulsion system for deep-space exploration. The device on which they are working is called the Hall Effect Rocket with Magnetic Shielding (HERMeS). The device can generate three times greater thrust than existing systems. NASA has identified this high-power solar electric propulsion system as a critical part of its deep-space exploration initiative. In March 2017, NASA ground-tested in a vacuum chamber (to imitate conditions in space) the electric propulsion system that is being developed.

PRACTICAL PROBLEMS OF INTERSTELLAR SPACE TRAVEL

Even if the problem of developing a means of propelling a starship across the vast distances of space at adequate speed were solved, there would remain a host of issues related to the survival of the people who will travel on the ship.

INTERSTELLAR SPACE FALLACIES

Sci-fi movies often ignore the laws of physics when they prove inconvenient. Here are five fallacies related to interstellar space travel often found in movies and television science fiction:

1. Traveling faster than the speed of light allows fictional spacecraft to get from one point to another with extreme rapidity. In reality, it is not possible to travel faster than the speed of light by journeying through space, and even near-light-speed travel would take days, weeks, or months to get to the destination.

2. One can't generate artificial gravity without spinning the ship to create centrifugal force. Not only do sci-fi movie spaceships apparently have a magic "gravity generator" that creates artificial gravity without generating centrifugal force, but when the power fails, gravity continues to operate in most cases. The exception is the ship in *2001: A Space Odyssey,* which got this fact correct.

3. Crew members don't experience the effects of inertia when accelerating or decelerating. In other words, someone says "Warp 15, ensign," and the ship accelerates from zero to near the speed of light instantaneously, but no one on board is pressed back by the force.

(continued on the next page)

(continued from the previous page)

4. People on spaceships traveling near, or even faster than, the speed of light carry on radio communications with people on other ships, on other planets, or back home at their headquarters. Instantaneous communication across light-year distances is not possible. Even when the NASA Mission Control Center in Houston talked to astronauts heading for the moon, there was a time lag between sending and receiving; over light-year distances, having a conversation would be impossible.

5. Spaceships travel through space continuously at near light speed without experiencing any damage. In reality, even the tiny atoms in space that the spaceship hits as it travels at enormous speed would create wear and tear on the ship.

All these conventions make science fiction more engaging and exciting, but they violate scientific laws.

SURVIVAL IN SPACE

Spaceships need power both for propulsion and for the systems within the ship. To generate power for internal systems, a ship might be able to use solar power and/or processed waste. However, propulsion systems are going to need fuel. How will interstellar travelers replenish this fuel? How will they obtain raw materials to make replacement parts and clothing? The ship will also need to contain an environment that can nourish and sustain generations of travelers for decades or centuries. People cannot live their lives in

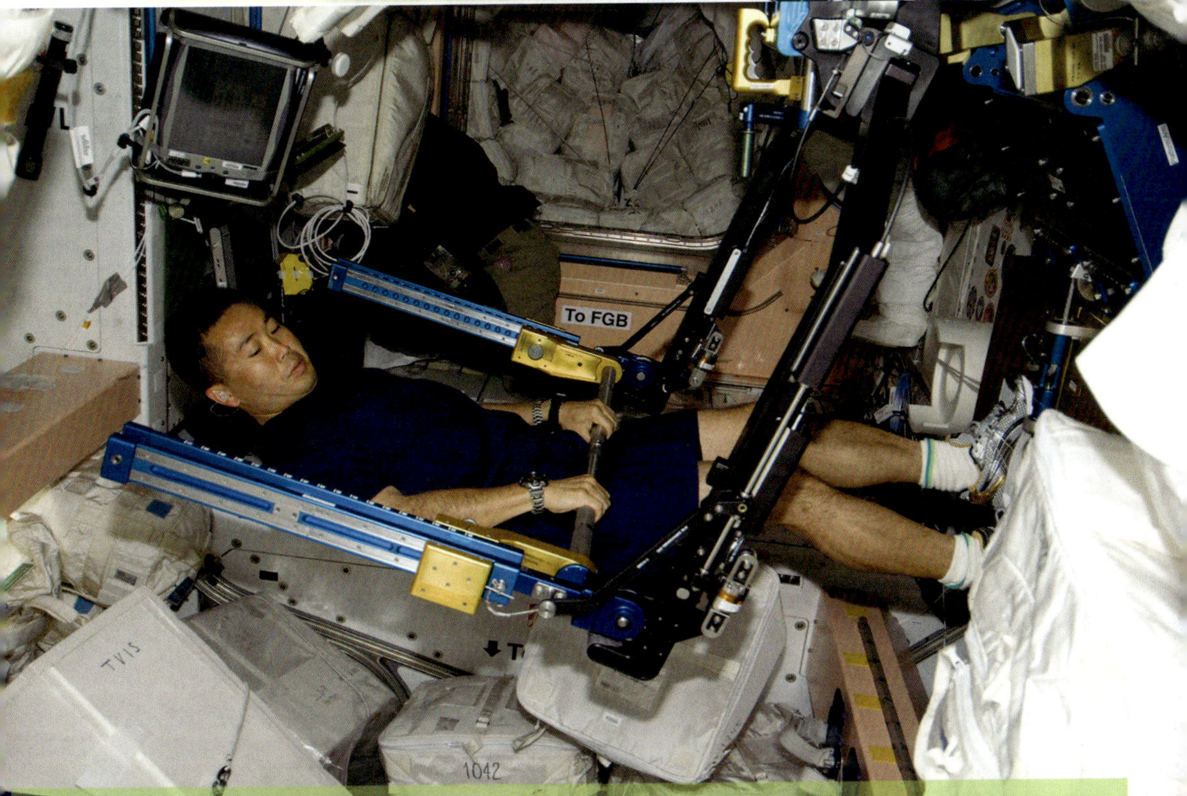

Maintaining one's muscles in weightless conditions, as astronaut Koichi Wakata is doing on the International Space Station, requires regular exercise, only one of many health issues that need to be addressed in interstellar travel.

a sterile environment like that shown in most movie spaceships. To thrive, they need sunlight and a calming environment. Otherwise, they are likely to suffer the types of mental stress and depression common in inmates in prisons. A ship would need to have "green parklike areas." Future generations might adapt to a space environment, developing characteristics that make them more suitable for travel in space, such as a resistance to radiation and a physiology better suited to low gravity. However, the first generation has to survive first. Human bodies are designed to live in Earth gravity. When human beings live in space, within weeks to months their bones become brittle, their muscles weaken, and their eyesight deteriorates. Years in space would permanently damage a person's body. Gravity can be created via centrifugal force by rotating the spaceship rapidly. This action has the short-term disadvantage of causing nausea and the long-term disadvantage of requiring a lot of energy. Human beings living on a spaceship need to eat, drink, and breathe. Because taking enough food, water, and air along for a journey of years or decades is impractical, the ship will have to be a complete ecosystem.

PROTECTION

A major problem of space travel is exposure to radiation. Ships need shielding to protect their human cargo. It could be lead shielding, but this type would be enormously heavy. Another approach involves generating electromagnetic shields around the ship to protect the people inside from cosmic radiation. The concept is based on the fact that electromagnetic fields can be used to deflect electrically charged objects. Magnetic fields could also function as "sails" on interplanetary missions. A strong magnetic shield could also be used as a sail to catch the plasma that occurs naturally in the solar and interstellar wind.

REPRODUCTION

Being in space affects the human body, including its hormones, the chemicals produced by the glands in the body that control bodily functions. Certain hormones are necessary for reproduction. Multigenerational ships are often suggested as the solution to interstellar travel. Mating is possible anywhere, but it remains to be seen whether a child can be conceived, carried to term, and born in space without birth defects. This issue is currently being studied by Japan on the International Space Station. In the "Space Pup" experiment, they are using mice to study the effects of space on mammalian fertility.

Obviously, there is a great deal more to achieving successful interstellar travel than firing up an advance propulsion system, loading the ship with people, and zooming off to a distant star. Solving the propulsion system problems is only the beginning to addressing all the issues that must be resolved to achieve a successful interstellar mission.

CHAPTER 4

THERE'S MORE TO SPACEFLIGHT THAN A GOOD ENGINE

The greatest challenge posed by interstellar space travel is not technical. It is the human beings who travel on the starship. Unlike machines, people have different values and views, skills, and status. They would be a community of individuals living out their lives in space. Further, they would be embarking on a one-way trip. Given the nature of interstellar space travel—traveling far from home for years, or even generations, in an insular community—ethical dilemmas are bound to arise.

THE CHOSEN FEW

The reason that people embark on an interstellar voyage would make a difference. In science fiction, interstellar ships are often used to save people from disaster on Earth. Because everyone can't go, there is a question of who does. Will interstellar travel be only for the rich and important in such a case? One clear problem with this approach is that it is obviously unfair to those who are left behind. A second problem is that the rich and powerful are probably not the best suited for creating a community on another planet. All one has to do is watch an episode of the CBS reality TV series *Undercover Boss* to see that, although they may be skilled in strategic planning, those at the top often lack the practical skills needed for day-to-day labor. When the Pilgrims arrived in Massachusetts, they survived their first winter only because of the assistance of friendly Native Americans. In *Eating in America: A History*, the authors, Waverley Root and Richard de Rochemont, make the following point about the Pilgrims who settled in America: "The first English-speaking colonists of America were not quite the right persons to wring a living from a wilderness … What the situation called for was lumberjacks or peasants or laborers, men and women accustomed to working with their hands and with their backs. What it got, both in the North and the South, was refugees from the middle class." They go on to say that those who came over on the *Mayflower* were mostly merchants, industrialists, shopkeepers, artisans, and small landowners who used hired help to farm their land—people who could afford the passage. In other words, they were the same types of people who in an emergency are most likely to be able to use their money or political influence to get a berth on a starship leaving Earth.

When the survival of the human race is at stake, should the people leaving on the starships be those with money and status or those with practical skills? Or should they be selected by lottery—and in this case what happens if no one is chosen who

A lottery wheeling system produces combinations of a range of numbers and guarantees winners in lottery games. Would using a lottery system be the fairest way to choose colonists for interstellar travel? Would it be the best method?

has a particular skill that is critical for survival? What happens if people are chosen who are likely to be disruptive—say a person who is racist? Should the chosen represent the distribution of races, ethnicities, or religions on Earth? On the other hand, could interstellar spaceflight be used to offload "less desirable" people? Would "colonization" become a means of getting rid of people deemed to be a problem for society, as was the case in the seventeenth century, when criminals and other undesirables were sent to the colonies in America and Australia?

FUTURE GENERATIONS

Multigenerational ships present a variety of ethical issues. For one thing, the multigenerational approach to spaceflight depends on the first generation being willing to breed the next generation. The first generation may be committed to this approach in advance. However, subsequent

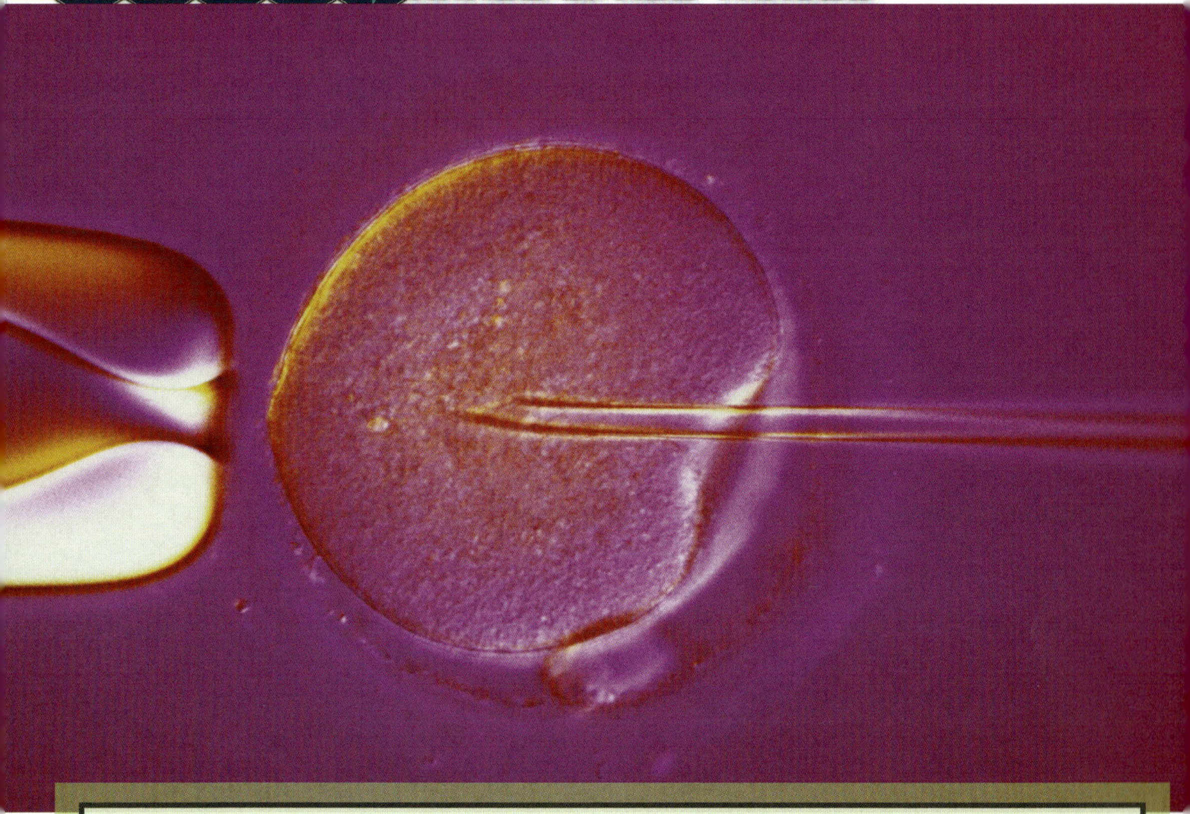

In this method of in-vitro insemination, a single sperm is injected into an egg cell by using a microneedle. In-vitro insemination and genetic engineering could be two approaches to raising future generations on a multigenerational ship.

generations will have to do so whether they want to or not—or the mission will fail. To avoid the problems of inbreeding, the choices of mates may have to be controlled. Alternately, new generations could be created from sperm and eggs in a laboratory, but this method also creates ethical, as well as psychological, dilemmas. Who will be responsible for raising the children? The egg and sperm donors will not necessarily be couples. Will the children develop psychological problems if they don't have a family and are raised in a group situation? The temptation to use genetic engineering to create children better adapted to live in space might be irresistible. Would these "superior" human beings be treated differently from "regular" people? Will they feel superior to nonengineered human beings?

Future generations will also be expected to carry on the mission, whether they want to or not. This notion may mean people will be forced to undertake occupations required to keep the mission viable, rather than pursuing their own interests. Essentially, the future generations will be indentured by their ancestors without their consent. It is not just children who present ethical quandaries. What happens when people age? Resources and living space are both limited on a starship. On a mission that depends on producing offspring, women of childbearing age are the priority. What happens to those whose children are grown and who are beyond childbearing age? People in their fifties and sixties have skills and are still able to work, but what happens when they become unable to work? Once they are no longer able to contribute skills or children to the mission, should limited resources and space be expended on them? Men can continue to father children beyond the age when most women have ceased to be fertile. Will competition to reproduce arise between established, powerful older men and younger men? What form will such competition take? Will it result in conflict or violence in the community?

THE ECONOMICS OF INTERSTELLAR SPACEFLIGHT

Implementing interstellar space travel will be expensive. There are advantages to exploring distant galaxies, among them advancing basic science, acquiring new materials, and spreading humanity to other

A DIFFERENT BREED: THE PSYCHOLOGICAL RESULTS OF INTERSTELLAR SPACE TRAVEL

Living on a ship either as a first-generation passenger or a member of a subsequent generation will affect people psychologically. The first generation that goes into space will still be "earthlings," with a culture and values that relate to their lives on Earth. The second generation will have parents who attempt to instill the same values in them. However, as generations come and go, the culture will change. People will no longer be Earth people in space. They will be space people. The second and subsequent generations will never have seen Earth. Hundreds of years after a ship has left Earth, the people will have developed their own way of speaking—accent, vocabulary, and dialect. This difference in language will likely be equivalent to the difference between the English of Shakespeare's day and that of the twenty-first century. People's beliefs, technology, and culture will also be different.

Being in the equivalent of an isolated small town will create stress. People may develop psychological problems. How will such people be treated? Eventually, most people will be related to some degree to everyone else, even if the relation is distant. How will this connection affect their interactions? Will they feel constrained in their behavior or rebellious? Will people become more willing to look out for one another, or will they break down into opposing groups along ethnic or religious lines, as happens when a large group of inmates is incarcerated in prison for years?

planets in case people destroy this one. Exploring space means using money that could be employed to address terrestrial needs. It is unlikely that the US government, already dealing with a large financial deficit, is going to pour huge amounts of money into interstellar travel—unless something occurs that forces them to do so, such as fear that the Earth is doomed and people might need to escape, or the fear that another major power is making advances in interstellar space travel that would put the United States at a scientific or military disadvantage. There are private companies that are exploring space travel, such as SpaceX, headed by Elon Musk, who has a plan to colonize Mars. Private companies engage in enterprises from which they can make a profit. Although the first commercial activities of private companies may be tourism in space, launching satellites, and facilitating scientific experimentation, they may become interested in pursuing commercial space-based enterprises in the future. If one relies on private enterprise, should these businesses be allowed to exploit new planets if they are discovered?

THOSE LEFT BEHIND

There is an inherent burden placed on the people of the country that sends an interstellar ship or ships on a long-term voyage that

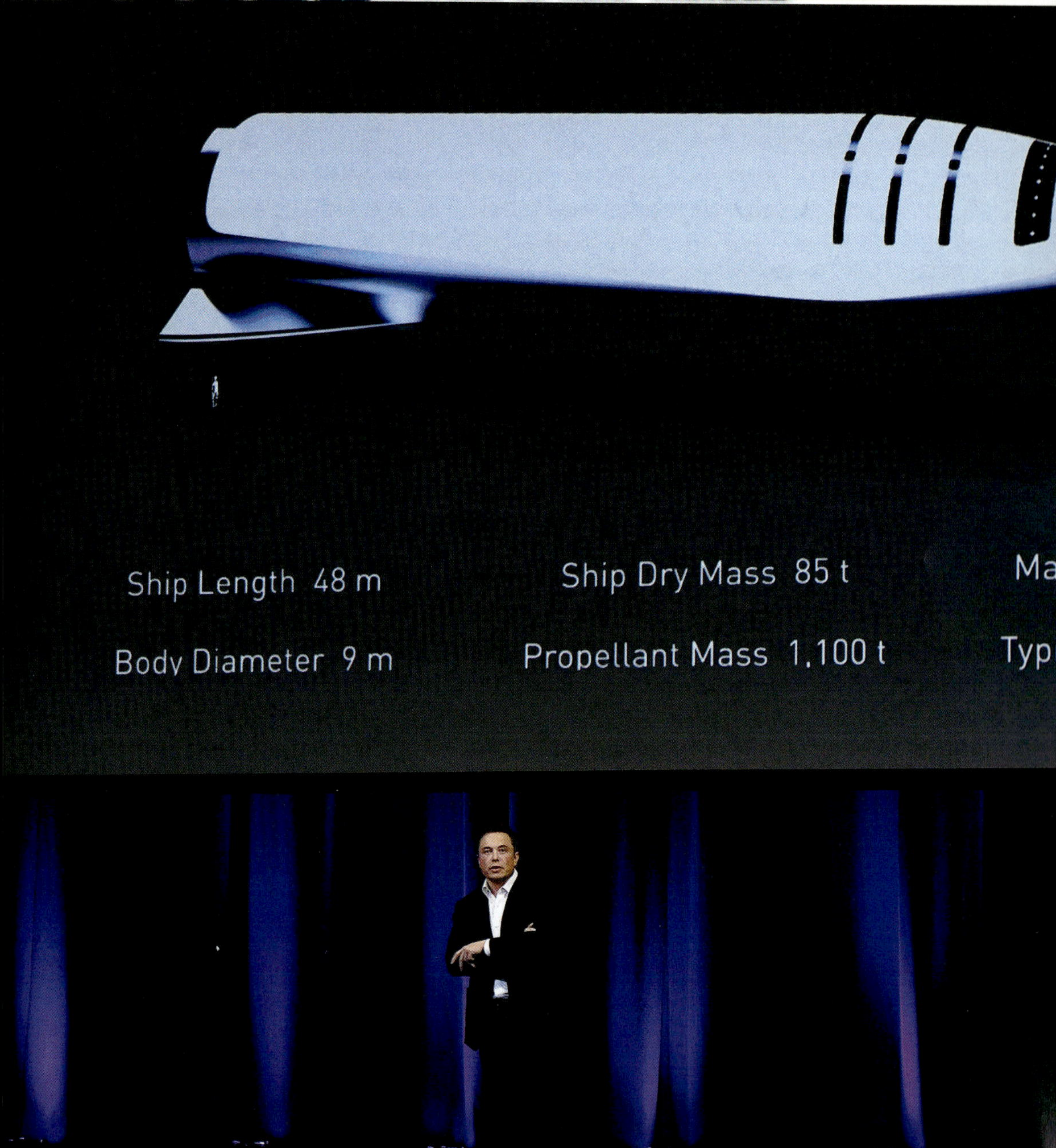

In September 2017, Elon Musk, chief executive officer of SpaceX, addressed the long-term technical challenges that need to be solved to achieve a self-sustaining colony on Mars. He also explained the Big Falcon Rocket design.

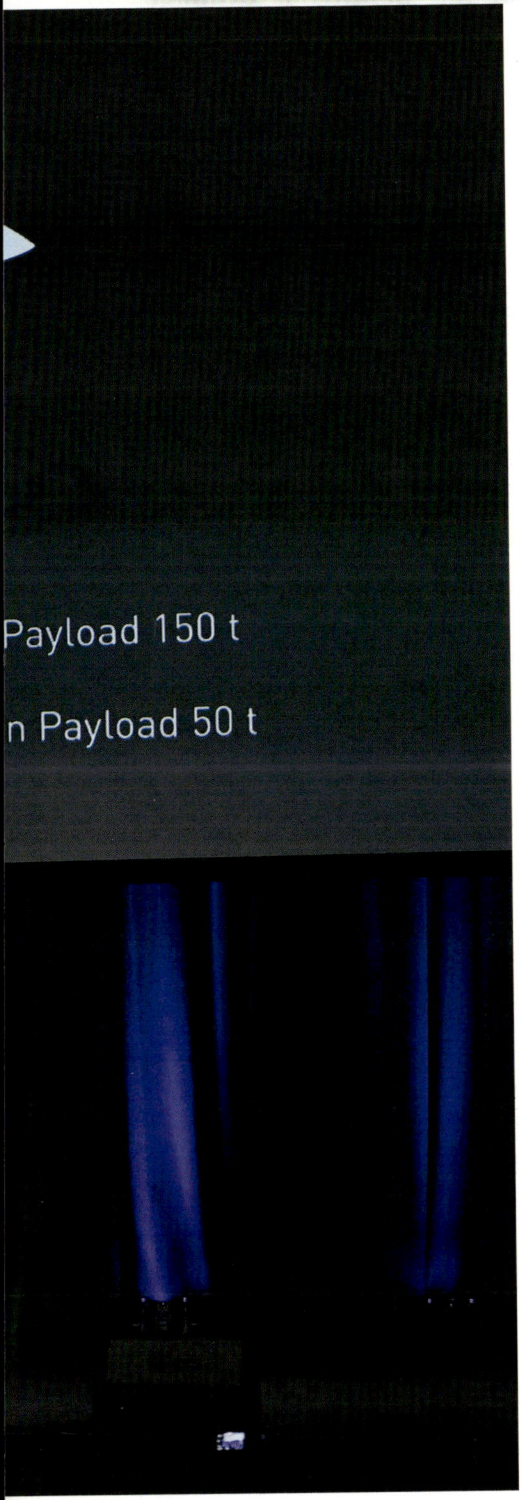

might take decades or even centuries. Such a project requires a lengthy commitment to maintaining the infrastructure to track and support the enterprise and pass on the information from one generation of workers to another. Again, this enterprise requires a very long commitment to continue to provide funds for the project at the expense of other possible areas of spending. In the more immediate sense, there is the question of whether the initial travelers will be scientists or colonists. Will a military presence be required? If scientists or military personnel go, will they leave their families behind? (Even if they are single, they may, for example, have parents who may need support at some point.) Therefore, the mission may require a commitment to the families of the people who are chosen to go. Will taxpayers and the government maintain this long-term commitment?

Since the turn of the last century, science fiction writers have speculated about traveling beyond

Interstellar space travel research provides opportunities to be part of the exploration of a new frontier. Here, a Delta IV Heavy rocket with the unmanned spacecraft *Orion* mounted at the top is ready for a test launch in 2014.

the solar system. Science and technology have reached the point where researchers are actively investigating concepts for interstellar travel. Of course, humans are still years off from undertaking a mission that goes beyond the Milky Way galaxy. However, the research and experimentation that could lead to such voyages are being performed today and could provide exciting opportunities for the young scientists and engineers of tomorrow. Interstellar manned space travel also raises a variety of questions that will need to be addressed.

TIMELINE

1638 British historian Francis Godwin publishes *The Man in the Moone.*

1911 F. W. Mader publishes *Wunderwelten*, in which a crew of young astronauts uses faster-than-light speed to travel to Alpha Centauri.

1947 Frederick Reines and Stanislaw Ulam, working on the Manhattan Project at Los Alamos National Laboratory, formulate the calculations for a nuclear-bomb-powered spacecraft, whose development would eventually become the Orion Project.

1961 On April 12, Russian cosmonaut Yuri Gagarin becomes the first human being in space, completing an orbit of Earth in *Vostok 1*.

1966 The TV series *Star Trek* premieres, featuring interstellar travel via warp drive.

1968 Arthur C. Clarke publishes *2001: A Space Odyssey*, describing a scientifically based deep spacecraft.

1969 On July 20, the *Apollo 11* lunar module lands on the moon and astronaut Neil Armstrong walks on its surface.

1977 The United States launches the *Voyager 1* deep space probe.

2000 The first permanent crew takes up residence in the International Space Station.

2004 On June 21, Virgin Galactic's *SpaceShipOne* becomes the first privately funded manned space vehicle to achieve suborbital flight.

2010 The US Defense Advanced Research Projects Agency (DARPA) and the National Aeronautics and Space Administration (NASA) initiate the 100 Year Starship grant project to encourage private entities to develop an interstellar spacecraft.

2012 A SpaceX commercial spacecraft successfully delivers cargo to the International Space Station.

2014 The European Space Agency's Rosetta probe completes a ten-year, four-billion-mile (6,437,376,000 km) journey, arriving at comet 67P/Churyumov–Gerasimenko.

In December, NASA test launches a Delta IV Heavy rocket with an uncrewed *Orion*.

2015 On March 6, NASA's *Dawn* spacecraft enters orbit around the dwarf planet Ceres in the asteroid belt between Mars and Jupiter.

On July 14, NASA's *New Horizon* spacecraft arrives at Pluto.

2017 In July, NASA's astronauts test *Orion* in the Gulf of Mexico to examine exit procedures in case of an emergency after splashing down.

On September 29, Elon Musk, founder of SpaceX, announces his revised rocket and spaceship designs for a colonization plan of Mars.

2019 NASA plans a test mission, called EM-1, for its Space Launch System and an uncrewed *Orion*.

2021 NASA's EM-2 will test some new propulsion systems and include a crew of astronauts on *Orion*.

2030 NASA plans to have a mission to Mars with a crew of astronauts by this date.

GLOSSARY

ambient Occurring in the environment where an object or person is located.

Cold War The period from the end of World War II until 1989 when the United States and the Soviet Union were engaged in an economic and political rivalry accompanied by a nuclear standoff.

cryogenics The technology used to freeze people for revival at a later time.

deficit In financial terms, when the amount of money being spent exceeds the amount of money being received.

dialect A local variation in speech and word usage.

fission The process of breaking atoms apart to release energy. It is the means by which conventional nuclear reactors operate.

fusion The process of compressing, or fusing, atoms together, which releases energy.

galactic Relating to our solar system.

global positioning system (GPS) A system of navigational satellites that can be accessed by vehicles such as planes and cars.

hibernation A sleeplike state in which the body's processes slow down significantly.

inertia The tendency of a body in motion to remain in motion and a body at rest to remain at rest.

insular Isolated as if on an island.

interstellar Relating to travel between star systems.

in-vitro insemination A process in reproduction in which a sperm cell is injected into an egg cell in a laboratory.

photon A particle of light.

physiology The study of the functioning of the body.

plasma A state of matter between gas and liquid.

proliferate To multiply greatly.

psychological Related to the functioning of the mind.

quandary A puzzle or dilemma.

quantum The smallest, indivisble unit of energy.

satirist A person who pokes fun at a subject to make a point.

solar wind The stream of particles emitted by the sun that travel through space the way that air particles travel through our atmosphere as wind.

speed of light The measurement 299,792,458 meters per second or 186,282 miles per second; the theoretical limit for how fast an object can travel.

suspended animation A state in which a person's vital bodily functions cease to operate but from which he or she can be revived.

symbiotic Mutually beneficial.

teleportation The theoretical means of immediately traveling between two locations without physically crossing the space in between them.

wormhole A theoretical tunnel through space created by warping spacetime.

FOR MORE INFORMATION

British Interplanetary Society (BIS)
Arthur C. Clarke House
27-29 South Lambeth Road
London SW8 1SZ
United Kingdom
44 (0) 20 7735 3160
Website: http://www.bis-space.com
Facebook: @bis.space
Twitter: @BIS_spaceflight
The BIS promotes the exploration of space. It publishes the magazine *Spaceflight*.

Canadian Space Agency (CSA)
John H. Chapman Space Centre
6767 Route de l'Aéroport
Saint-Hubert, QC J3Y 8Y9
Canada
(450) 926-4800
Website: http://www.asc-csa.gc.ca/eng/Default.asp
Facebook: @CanadianSpaceAgency
Instagram: @canadianspaceagency
Twitter: @csa_asc
CSA is the agency for overseeing Canada's space exploration and astronomical activities.

European Space Agency (ESA)
Fermi Ave
Harwell, Didcot OX11 0FD
United Kingdom
Website: http://www.esa.int
The European Space Agency is an organization composed of twenty-two European member states, and its mission is to promote the exploration of space. ESA's website features the latest news in space exploration, including human spaceflight.

National Aeronautics and Space Administration (NASA)
300 E. Street SW, Suite 5R30
Washington, DC 20546
(202) 358-0001
Website: https://www.nasa.gov
Twitter: @NASA
NASA is the agency that administers and oversees the US space program; its website provides information on its current and future missions.

SpaceX
Rocket Road
Hawthorne, CA
Website: http://www.spacex.com
(310) 363-6000
Facebook, Twitter, and YouTube: @SpaceX
SpaceX designs, manufactures, and launches advanced

rockets and spacecraft. The private company was founded in 2002 to revolutionize space technology, with the ultimate goal of enabling people to live on other planets.

Virgin Galactic
4022 E Conant Street
Long Beach, CA 90808-1777
(562) 384-4400
Website:
http://www.virgingalactic.com
Facebook, Instagram, and Twitter:
@virgingalactic
Virgin Galactic is a company that is pioneering tourism in space. It is working toward offering the world's first commercial spaceline.

United Nations Office for Outer Space Affairs (UNOOSA)
United Nations Office at Vienna
Vienna International Centre
Wagramerstrasse 5
A-1220 Vienna
Austria
+43-1-260 60 4950
Website: http://www.unoosa.org
Facebook and Twitter:
@UNOOSA
Instagram: @unoosa
UNOOSA is the United Nations office responsible for promoting international cooperation in the peaceful uses of outer space, including maintaining a registry of objects in space and providing educational information and technical advice.

FOR FURTHER READING

Bova, Ben, with Anthony Lewis. *Space Travel—A Science Fiction Writer's Guide.* Golden, CO: ReAnimus Press, 2012.

Brake, Mark, and Jon Chase. *The Science of Star Wars: The Scientific Facts Behind the Force, Space Travel, and More!* New York, NY: Racehorse Publishing, 2016.

Clarke, Arthur C. *2001: A Space Odyssey.* 1968. Reprint, New York, NY: Penguin, 2016.

Editors of Popular Science. *The Future of Space Travel.* New York, NY: Time Inc. Books, 2017.

Felix, Rebecca. *12 Things to Know about Space Exploration.* North Mankato, MN: 12-Story Library, 2015.

Goldstein, Margaret J. *Private Space Travel: A Space Discovery Guide.* Minneapolis, MN: Lerner Publishing, 2017.

Haley, Guy. *Sci-Fi Chronicles: A Visual History of the Galaxy's Greatest Science Fiction.* Buffalo, NY: Firefly Press, 2014.

Miller, Ron. *Spaceships: An Illustrated History of the Real and the Imagined.* Washington, DC: Smithsonian Books, 2016.

Montross, Sarah J. *Past Futures: Science Fiction, Space Travel, and Postwar Art of the Americas.* Cambridge, MA: MIT Press, 2015.

Odenwald, Sten. *Interstellar Travel: An Astronomer's Guide.* Self-published: CreateSpace Publishing, 2015.

Tyson, Neil deGrasse. *StarTalk: Everything You Ever Need to Know About Space Travel, Sci-Fi, the Human Race, the Universe, and Beyond.* Washington, DC: National Geographic, 2016.

BIBLIOGRAPHY

Alpert, Mark. "Warp Drive Research Key to Interstellar Travel." *Scientific American*, April 23, 2014. https://blogs.scientificamerican.com/guest-blog/warp-drive-research-key-to-interstellar-travel.

Anders, Charlie Jane. "10 Myths About Space Travel That Make Science Fiction Better." io9, August 22, 2012. https://io9.gizmodo.com/5936924/10-myths-about-space-travel-that-make-science-fiction-better.

Asimov, Isaac. *The Currents of Space.* New York, NY: Fawcett Crest, 1953.

Asimov, Isaac. "The Truth Isn't Stranger Than Science Fiction—Just Slower." *The New York Times*, February 12, 1984. http://www.nytimes.com/books/97/03/23/lifetimes/asi-v-truth.html?mcubz=1.

Baxter, Stephen. "The Spaceships of Arthur C. Clarke." Space.com, July 27, 2016. https://www.space.com/33537-spacecraft-of-arthur-c-clarke-stephen-baxter.html.

Brin, David. *Insistence of Vision.* Stamford, CT: Storytime Books, 2016.

Brown, David W. "5 Fictional Ways to Go Very Fast in Space." Mental Floss, January 8, 2013. http://mentalfloss.com/article/32146/5-fictional-ways-go-very-fast-space.

David, Leonard. "NASA's 100-Year Starship Project Sets Sights on Interstellar Travel." Space.com, March 23, 2011. https://www.space.com/11200-nasa-100-year-starship-interstellar-travel.html.

Embry-Riddle Aeronautical University. "Methods for Practical Space Travel and Exploration," Retrieved September 13, 2017. http://pages.erau.edu/~andrewsa/RavProjectSpaceTravel.html.

European Space Agency (ESA). "Innovative Technologies from Science Fiction for Space Applications." Retrieved September 11, 2017. http://www.esa.int/esapub/br/br176/br176.pdf.

Flora, Michael. "Project Orion: Its Life, Death, and Possible Rebirth." Retrieved September 19, 2017. http://www.islandone.org/Propulsion/ProjectOrion.html.

Fraknol, Andrew. "Science Fiction Stories with Good Astronomy & Physics: A Topical Index." Astronomical Society of the Pacific, October 2015. https://www.astrosociety.org/education

/astronomy-resource-guides/science-fiction-stories-with-good -astronomy-physics-a-topical-index/#travel.

Friedman, Louis. *Human Spaceflight: From Mars to the Stars.* Tucson, AZ: University of Arizona Press, 2015.

Hollingham, Richard. "Interstellar Travel: Raising Children in Space." BBC Future, May 27, 2014. http://www.bbc.com/future /story/20140527-raising-a-family-in-space.

Letzter, Rafi. "Interstellar Travel Won't Look Anything Like the Movie." *Popular Science*, October 28, 2014. http://www.popsci.com /article/technology/interstellar-travel-wont-look-anything-movie.

Mulcahy, Kate. "Top 10 Problems with Interstellar Travel." Listverse, February 27, 2012. http://listverse.com/2012/02/27/top-10 -problems-with-interstellar-travel.

NASA. "Electric Propulsion Will Thrust Exploration into Deep Space," March 13, 2017. https://www.nasa.gov/image-feature/electric -propulsion-will-thrust-exploration-into-deep-space.

Nogrady, Bianca. "The Myths and Reality about Interstellar Space Travel." BBC, October 4, 2016. http://www.bbc.com/future /story/20161003-the-myths-and-reality-about-interstellar-travel.

Pohl, Frederik. *The Gold at the Starbow's End.* New York, NY: Ballantine, 1972.

Root, Waverley, and Richard de Rochemont. *Eating in America: A History.* New York, NY: The Ecco Press, 1981.

Santa Barbara City College. "History of Science Fiction Films." Retrieved September 12, 2017. https://soma.sbcc.edu/users/davega/NON _ACTIVE_CLASSES/FILMST_118/GENRE/ScienceFiction /History%20of%20science%20fiction%20films.pdf.

INDEX

ABOUT THE AUTHOR

Jeri Freedman has a bachelor of arts degree from Harvard University. For fifteen years, she has been working at high-technology companies. She is the author of numerous young adult nonfiction books, including *Robots through History*, as well as being the coauthor, under the name Ellen Foxxe, of two science fiction fantasy novels.

PHOTO CREDITS

Cover, p. 1 Corbis Historical/Getty Images; pp. 4, 7, 20, 29, 42 NikoNomad/Shutterstock.com; p. 5 Found Image Holdings Inc/Corbis Historical/Getty Images; pp. 8, 33, 52 NASA; p. 10 Universal Images Group/Getty Images; p. 12 Victor Habbick/Shutterstock.com; p. 16 AF Archive/Alamy Stock Photo; p. 19 Archive Photos/Moviepix/Getty Images; p. 21 Courtesy Everett Collection; p. 23 Adam Gasson/Getty Images; p. 24 Bettmann/Getty Images; p. 26 Victor Habbick Visions/Science Photo Library/Getty Images; p. 31 Hulton Archive/Archive Photos/Getty Images; p. 35 Education Images/Universal Images Group/Getty Images; p. 39 Handout/Getty Images; pp. 44–45 Gerardo Burmester/EyeEm/Getty Images; p. 46 Spike Walker/The Image Bank/Getty Images; pp. 50–51 Mark Brake/Getty Images; back cover and interior pages (circular element), interior pages (grid and circuit board patterns) Titima Ongkantong/Shutterstock.com.

Design: Nelson Sá; Layout: Tahara Anderson; Senior Editor: Kathy Kuhtz Campbell; Photo Researcher: Nicole Baker